Brilliant on the Skyline
General Aviation Terminal Schiphol

Author
Marina de Vries
With contributions by
Ad Rutten and Jan Benthem

Photography
Jeroen Musch

SUN architecture Publishers

Robust, Refined and Rosy

Ad Rutten

Schiphol-East is where today's airport began. This is the place where the first airplanes landed at the beginning of the last century and where the first wooden terminal stood. For some time now, Schiphol-East has been the terrain of hangars and private airplanes. We have had the privilege of welcoming many famous people from all over the world on this spot: Jayne Mansfield, Martin Luther King, The Beatles, U2, to mention a few. More and more, however, general aviation is embracing the corporate world, and Schiphol-East is becoming the home base for business jets.

Seen from Schiphol-East, the skyline of our Airport City is at its most beautiful; one can see the tower, terminal, taxiing planes and the ascending and alighting flights. Nevertheless, Schiphol-East is separate from the buzz of the millions of passengers at Schiphol-Centre. Here, the focus is still on small-scale, exclusivity and the magic of general aviation. Schiphol-East is full of history, and that is what makes this area so special.

Schiphol-East, nonetheless, also keeps up with the times. Indeed, it wants to be a forerunner. The previous terminal for general aviation was authentic but obsolete and no longer adequate. Now we have a new GA Terminal*) which is robust, refined and rosy. An eye-catching presence in the landscape, like a presumptuous little brother, GA Terminal taunts the big terminal at Schiphol-Centre. I can say in all honesty that GA Terminal can compete with the finest terminals I have seen in the world. The terminal exudes an air of pure flying pleasure, a feeling that because of its special location at the top of the landing strip is apparent everywhere, even in the offices.

The new GA Terminal adds another chapter to the contemporary history and reputation of our airport. The development of Schiphol is based on good architecture and a vision that takes into account future generations of passengers. The terminal at Schiphol-Centre was designed over a half-century ago, but despite all the changes that have occurred in aviation, it still accommodates – albeit with a few modifications – one of the best aviation processes in Europe. Now, general aviation has also acquired quarters which measure up to that.

The design is not only daring but extremely functional. The terminal's overhang welcomes the airplanes with outstretched arms. Heads of state and rock stars can comfortably set foot on the ground here and then quickly and stylishly step into their cars. Thanks to the terminal's smooth handling setup business passengers can board their planes in no time.

Our new GA Terminal is, just like its big brother Schiphol-Centre once was, far ahead of its time. Schiphol is now Europe's preferred airport for general aviation. We are extremely proud about that. So, bring on the most exclusive passengers of them all: we are ready, as are KLM, Jet Support and Aviapartner, our handling agents.

Ad Rutten is Executive Vice President and Chief Operational Officer of Schiphol Group

*) General aviation (GA) is one of the two categories of civil aviation. It refers to all flights other than military and scheduled airline and regular cargo flights, both private and commercial.

The Bold and Adventurous Feeling of Pure Flying

Jan Benthem

Every general aviation flyer knows the tingle of excitement that comes when heading towards the airplane. This has to do with all of the preparations, of course, and with flying itself, but also with the charm of the terrain on which this small form of aviation usually takes place – in a shed or hangar, on the sidelines of large aviation. Here, the sensation of flying still exists.

That real feeling of flying is still present at Schiphol-East. As young architects thirty years ago, Mels Crouwel and I were already doing small jobs at Schiphol-East. We designed electricity substations and a temporary bus station, and when the airport was demolishing redundant facilities, argued for the preservation of the original control tower to be the heart of the area and a memento of the glorious past. In a later urban development plan for Schiphol-East, we made sure that it was still possible to have a view of the flights and central platform from the industrial buildings, and from between the operational and logistic buildings. This is why I'm pleased that this special spot – looking out at the former grass field where the very first planes landed and took off and where Schiphol originated – is where the GA Terminal has been built. As a building, the GA Terminal has nothing in common with the large terminal. The latter is all about handling a large number of passengers in the most efficient possible manner. The smaller GA Terminal involves safety and border transactions, of course, but also a super-individual approach towards both pilots and passengers, and preserving the magic of flying.

The new GA Terminal does precisely what it is supposed to do. The building exudes that certain aura of freedom, of daring and of the Wild West – the 'Peter Stuyvesant feeling' as it used to be called in Holland, or the 'Marlboro feeling' as it is known in the USA. At the same time, it offers the glamour and level of luxury synonymous with private business jets. In airport architecture, every prediction of the future is overtaken by history. Thus not much can be said about the future of the GA Terminal, except for this. At a time of a tremendous increase in scale, when bigger and bigger airplanes and ever more passengers are necessitating radical decisions, I think it special that Schiphol has also invested in a hypermodern facility for smaller airplanes. I'm looking forward to the excitement of taking off from here in this magical place, in this building with the equally bold and adventurous feeling of pure flying – when I have some spare time again, and a plane of my own.

Jan Benthem is partner of Benthem Crouwel Architects and has been Chief Architect for Schiphol since 1988. He is a former airman and sport pilot.

Schiphol General Aviation
Amsterdam Airport

Aviation
66-LZ-VH

Schiphol-East, 1948. Airfield with KLM airplanes DC-3

Schiphol-East, 1951. Airfield with departing passengers on their way to Teheran.

Schiphol, 1950. A family arrives at the airfield by taxi.

Little girl fascinated by the huge propeller of an airplane.

Jane Mansfield walking the staircase at Schiphol airport, 1957.

Audrey Hepburn arriving from London, 1954.

Schiphol-East, 1956. Airfield with main building in the back

Schiphol-East, 1956

KLM
SHELL

Amsterdam Airport Schiphol, 1970.

KLM
KLM ROYAL DUTCH AIRLINES

Amsterdam Airport Schiphol, 1968

Amsterdam Airport Schiphol, 1971. Boeing 747 and DC 8

Private jet interior, Learjet 45 XR

Learjet 45 XR

Schiphol, 1990. Nelson Mandela touched Dutch ground for the first time in his life.

Schiphol-East, 2001. Arrival of Irish rock band U2 for a couple of performances in the Netherlands.

Schiphol, 1991. Arrival of James Brown, "Godfather of Soul", in the Netherlands.

Schiphol, 1997. Tower and main building in early in the morning.

Schiphol-
East,
2011.
Former
GA terminal
building.

Schiphol's General Aviation Terminal makes flying a magical experience again

Marina de Vries

Glamorous and Businesslike

Schiphol's General Aviation Terminal – where the private and business flights of heads of states, CEOs, members of the royal family, pop stars, top football players and private aircraft are handled – is a remarkable tour de force. The terminal subtly blends in with the business-chic and industrial environment of Schiphol-East. Yet, at the same time, the terminal distinguishes itself from the surrounding enterprises and hangars by radiating a sense of pleasure for flying. The new, small terminal is so distinctive that it can even be seen from its big brother at Schiphol-Centre due to its streamlined form and magenta-coloured overhang, its plating that glitters in the sun like a disco ball and its warm pink glow in the evening light. The GA Terminal at Schiphol is not only a glamorous building, it also liber-ates all aspects of flying from their harness of routine and necessary evil. 'Sitting is a verb', the one-liner by the famous Dutch architect Gerrit Rietveld (1888–1964), is history. In this GA Terminal, all of the ground functions – arriving, driving to the entrance, parking, checking in, waiting, sitting, taxiing down the runway – are elevated to magical experiences.

Whether it is entering the building through the drive-in without being bothered by rain or paparazzi, or waiting in one of the lounges at eye level with the cockpit of your own aircraft, or the contrast between the terminal's mysterious reflecting exterior and the panoramic view from inside, or seeing the dancing silhouette of your plane in the pink mirrored windows on takeoff or landing – it all unfolds naturally like the scenes of a film. The GA Terminal at Schiphol is an experience you will not easily forget.

Attention has also been given to the pilot's experience. He waits out of sight of the passengers in his own half-sunken domain, while he can watch his guests arriving from afar.

Multifunctional Terminal for Various Handling Agents

General Aviation – with Piaggios, Gulfstreams and Learjets holding a maximum of twenty passengers – might be the most ordinary business in the world in the United States with its countless millionaires, but in the Netherlands it is a stable niche market. This exclusive sector handles some 15,000 flights and 14,000 passengers a year, a fraction of the 400,000 flights and 45 million passengers handled annually by the regular aircraft at Schiphol. As a rule, GA Terminal is a relatively small building that resembles a chic office. Such new buildings, certainly in Europe, are rare.

Until July 2011, General Aviation was located in Building 106 at Schiphol Airport in Amsterdam, a part of the former, postwar main terminal that remained standing after the main airport was moved from Schiphol-East to Schiphol-Centre in the late 1960s. Since then, Schiphol-East has developed into a high-quality site dedicated to technology and offices.

Some 15 years ago, the need arose for a new General Aviation building as the old one had become inefficient and run-down. There were plans to relocate this segment elsewhere, until, around the turn of the century, society and business grew much more internationalized and the sector's importance increased. This required a properly functioning GA Terminal. After interviewing handling agents and operators, Schiphol Real Estate, which is responsible for business, office and area development at Schiphol and a number of other airport terrains abroad, came to the conclusion that the construction of a new building was feasible on the understanding that it would be a special building: a multifunctional terminal, designed for multiple handling agents in combination with offices, a showroom and parking.

Desire for the Magic of Flying

Keeping the functions and desires of the target group in mind, Schiphol Real Estate invited three Dutch architectural firms to present their vision of a new GA Terminal. The choice fell to VMX Architects. This Amsterdam-based firm had, at that point, completed a number of exceptional buildings. In addition to houses and schools, the temporary bicycle parking facility next to Amsterdam's central station and the bright purple offices of the Government Building Department Directie Noordzee in Rijswijk had already drawn a lot of attention. VMX's buildings are user-friendly, functional and sensational. Yet this architectural firm was chosen not for its designs but for its conceptual approach. This approach was what Schiphol Real Estate was looking for, because the brief for the GA Terminal needed to be developed collaboratively. Moreover, the ideas VMX presented were appealing, harking back to the excitement and glamour of the Golden Age of Aviation during the 1950s and 60s when greater leisure time and prosperity were accompanied by a rapid growth in air traffic, and when even going to an airport restaurant was a sensation. In the existing GA Terminal, the magic of flying, like in so many terminals nowadays, had been swept under a carpet of safety regulations. What is more, the building suffered from a number of other shortcomings, including long waiting queues for passengers who had to be bussed to their planes.

Slowly but surely the brief was put on the table. The new GA Terminal would be a model of flying pleasure, a glamorous, hospitable and comfortable building, with minimal walking distances and maximum privacy. The thrill of flying had to be palpable, down to every office. For these requirements and wishes, the location at the end of the runway was a gift.

Dutch Design as Calling Card

The initial design process for the new GA Terminal entailed an investigation into the history of the location and bespoke airport architecture at home and abroad. Schiphol had always been an innovative front-runner. In 1938, Schiphol was one of the first airports in Europe to have paved runways, and in the postwar years, the airport at Schiphol-East developed into the red carpet welcome to Holland. This was where celebrities and the royal family arrived, from film star Jayne Mansfield and Martin Luther King to Prince Bernhard. The public watched from spectacular terraces.

Upon its inauguration in 1967, Schiphol-Centre created a furore as one of the first passenger-friendly airports in the world. This was primarily due to its main terminal, designed by architect Marius Duintjer (1908–1983) and NACO (Netherlands Airport Consultants). The terminal was extraordinarily functional, conveniently arranged, elegant, as light and transparent as a 'doorzonwoning' (a Dutch house with windows at opposite ends of the lounge), and built to human scale. The interior was custom-made by Kho Liang Ie, and the clear yellow signposting was designed by Benno Wissing. Giving vital directions for passengers, the signposting was an example followed by countless airports. The later, modernized version of the signposting with added pictograms by Paul Mijksenaar is still imitated throughout the world.

Schiphol has always employed Dutch design talent to mark the airport as the gateway to the Netherlands, using architectural firms such as cepezed, Benthem Crouwel, Paul de Ruiter, Quist Wintermans and Broekbakema. The work of contemporary artists like Rob Birza, Tom Claassen and John Körmeling has also been incorporated to offer diversion and inspiration.

Nowadays the airport is making a name for itself as Airport City, a lively urban area with mixed functions, ranging from the terminal to business parks developed over the past few decades. The auxiliary branch of the Rijksmuseum beyond the passport checkpoint is unique, as is the recently inaugurated Airport Library and Airport Park. Schiphol is bringing in more and more Dutch Design. But no matter how much this largest of Dutch airports continues to modernize, Duintjer's terminal is indelibly printed in architects' memories, including that of VMX.

Plane in Front of the Door

The design team for GA Terminal – which besides VMX Architects and Schiphol Real Estate included design engineer Van Rossum and consulting engineer Nelissen, with the addition of building contractor Friso for construction – also looked at terminals across the Dutch borders. Anyone wishing to revive the Golden Age of Aviation inevitably will refer to the two striking terminals designed by the Finnish-American master builder Eero Saarinen (1910–1960) and both put into operation in 1962: TWA Terminal in New York and Dulles International Airport terminal in Chantilly, Virginia. These terminals celebrate the freedom attained through flying with expressive, flowing buildings. Fanning-out planes of glass offer panoramic views. In particular, the slanted shape of the windows and the relationship of the interior with the surrounding aviation landscape are reflected in the new GA Terminal, consciously or not.

Eero Saarinen, TWA Terminal in New York, 1962.

Eero Saarinen, Dulles International Airport in Chantilly, 1962.

In terms of essence, the new GA Terminal is first of all indebted to John Travolta's villa in Florida. The 'Pulp Fiction' film star lives in Jumbolair Aviation Estates near Ocala, a special community with houses built around a runway. Travolta's home has a driveway for cars on one side and two 'carports' for planes on the other. The comfort of this fly-in home, where passengers board the plane while staying out of the rain or sun thanks to a covered port and taxiway, became one of the most important starting points for the GA Terminal.

John Travolta's house in Florida

Pan Am Terminal of JFK Airport, 1960

Other terminals served as models for the shape of the overhang on the roof, including the grandly elegant overhang around the Pan Am Terminal at JFK Airport (designed by Ives, Turano & Gardner Associated Architects with Walter Prokosch of Tippetts-Abbett-McCarthy-Stratton, 1960) beneath which the airplanes are parked with their noses pointing toward the terminal, and the semi-circular, 40-meter-long roof of the Berlin Tempelhof Airport (Ernst Sagebiel, 1937) with its, then, extremely modern metal construction referring to the wing of an airplane.

Customized Down to Every Detail

However inspiring these terminals may be, none of them offered a ready-made answer to the specific brief of the GA Terminal at Schiphol. Slowly but surely, it was custom-designed to blend in perfectly with its location. As a result, it can be considered, with the advantage of hindsight, as a shining example of slow architecture, in which attention was also given to the surroundings comprised of familiar buildings made with dedication and rooted in their place.

The brief called for privacy, comfort, efficiency and openness as well as magic and glamour, but without nostalgia. This quickly led to a number of architectural solutions. Beneath a generous overhang, an airplane could park with its nose right up to the terminal, which in combination with the drive-in would allow passengers to board and disembark without being rained upon or exposed to curious glances. While walking distances for passengers have been kept to a minimum, the transparent spit-level setup has enabled as many spaces as possible to have a direct view of the spectacle from the airside. Moreover, by keeping the terminal open and unobstructed, both passengers and handling agents would have a total overview of the space, making it possible to keep the number of surveillance cameras to a minimum. Cameras would be present of course, but like all other necessary security measures, very inconspicuously.

The sculptural exterior was determined less quickly. In the first studies, like other designs by VMX and JFK Airport, the GA Terminal was round. In a second study it was square, with a straight overhang and a protruding drive-in structure. This design, however, proved too costly.

To meet the financial stipulations, an unorthodox solution was chosen. Instead of making the building smaller, it was enlarged, with more office space for handling agents and other interested parties. This made the logistic puzzle, already complicated due to the combination of aviation and non-aviation functions, even more complex. For how could the fervently desired privacy of the passengers be guaranteed now that smartphones had made paparazzi of us all? In order to prevent a direct view onto the parked airplanes from the offices situated above, the overhang was slanted upward. Long, open strips in the overhang would bring daylight into the offices and provide exciting views of the surrounding aviation landscape even when sitting at a desk. To gain extra square metres within the prescribed building and contour lines, the walls of the building were slanted outward on three sides, resulting in windows reminiscent of Saarinen. In this way, the design grew into a dynamic 3D diamond-shaped lozenge, customized to every detail.

The Roof Overhang as Red Carpet

Just as the striking form emerged from the brief, so did the colours and materials. They had to be simple and businesslike, in keeping with the location, but also sensual, glamorous and distinctive. The first impression given by the building is grey and shiny, in accordance with the aluminium colour prescribed by Benthem Crouwel's master plan for Schiphol. But the gray of the GA Terminal gives a cheeky wink to its surroundings. The specially developed panel system is speckled like a disco ball. In sunny weather, colours fly in all directions. Silver grey is also the colour of the mirrored glass of the huge slanted windows at landside. The mirrored glass keeps out curious glances and ensures privacy. At the same time, it strengthens the dynamics of the terminal by reflecting the wide, cloudy Dutch skies and the thrilling skyline of the airport like a continually changing painting.

But the unusual magenta colour of the overhang and the airside window panels is definitely what makes the GA Terminal recognizable in a million. Why pink, for heaven's sake? Seldom is there just one reason. For the overhang, Schiphol Real Estate wanted a colour that would be unique to Schiphol, a red tone that would underscore the special nature of the terminal and also make it visible from Schiphol-Centre. The colour of red came from the idea of a red carpet, the internationally recognized welcome for VIPs. This eventually turned into magenta, a mixture of the urbanity of the Cosmopolitan*, the pragmatism of the 'Het Financieele Dagblad' newspaper and the sportsmanship of the Giro d'Italia.

Pink is also the colour of 'girl glamour'. By using pink, the terminal is anticipates a future when general aviation will longer primarily be a man's world. Increasingly, women are being better represented in high business positions. They also form an important target group for general aviation. In the meantime, the GA Terminal at Schiphol is welcoming them. What's more, the wall of pink glass also bathes the world in a warm glow on grey Dutch weather days.

Jewel on the skyline

The GA Terminal not only sophisticatedly blends into its surroundings, it also refers to Schiphol's history and reputation in a contemporary manner all its own. In continuation with Duintjer, the terminal is conveniently arranged and efficient, light and transparent, elegant and carefully manicured down to the last detail. Just like some of the international terminals from the Golden Age, the GA Terminal celebrates the freedom and lightness of flying – in its flowing shape that, thanks to the recessed plinth, seems to float in the air, in its overhang construction referring to an airplane wing and in its sensual interweaving with the aviation landscape. What's more, it adds a new chapter. With its filmic principle and sensational use of materials, the GA Terminal is not only passenger friendly, it also offers a unique experience that is interrelated with the location.

Like the exterior, the customized interior radiates an atmosphere of optimism and glamour from the carefree age of aviation, with a modern note all its own. The counters designed by VMX, which repeat the shape of the terminal, are as simple as they are inventive, as functional as they are cosmopolitan. They are check-in point and cocktail bar at the same time. The same goes for the floors in the public areas. They all are laid with the same composite tile, but by cutting the tiles straight or diagonally, each area gains its own identity. The floor in the entrance hall lets there be no mistaking of the terminal's location: the snazzy windmill motif, an ode to the geometrical graphics of Escher (1898–1972), is Dutch with a twist.

Thanks to the creativity and input of all parties involved, the complex puzzle has been ingeniously solved. The GA Terminal shines like a jewel on the skyline and, with its 6000 square metres of gross floor surface, is no more costly than a standard office. Energy efficient thermal and electrical systems and motion detectors ensure its title as a 'sustainably good' design. Once again, a calling card for Dutch Design and building ingenuity has been produced.

Marina de Vries is a freelance journalist specializing in architecture and art. Her clients include the newspaper 'De Volkskrant', the 'Royal Institute of Dutch architects' (BNA), the magazine 'Hollands Diep' and the 'Virtual Museum Zuidas'. She has also collaborated on numerous publications, recently for the 'Amsterdam Medical Center.'

*)

The Cosmopolitan is a cocktail that became popular thanks to the American television series 'Sex and the City'. This glamorous and sensual cocktail can be made in various ways, including as follows:

- 2 measures vodka or tequila
- 1 measure cranberry juice
- ½ measure lemon juice
- a dash of triple sec (optional)
- shake with ice.

Martinair
Martinair
4 RUYS

Martinair
Martinair

17
18
19

1

Vertre

viation Terminal
trek

Project Information

General Aviation Terminal Schiphol

Functions
Airport terminal for private and business aviation, lounges, flight handling, office space. About 4,500 business jet flights and 15,000 passengers are handled at Schiphol-East per year.

Location
Amsterdam Airport Schiphol, Schiphol-East

Gross floor area
6,000 m²
of which:
1,000 m² terminal and lounges,
4,000 m² office space,
1,000 m² parking space (42 parking spaces)

Start of construction
December 2009

Delivery
April 2011

Operational
July 2011

Building partners

Investor and developer
Schiphol Real Estate

Pieter van der Horst
Frank Diepstraten
Martijn Horsman
Han Zeelen

Architect
VMX Architects

Don Murphy
Leon Teunissen
Hugo Kok

Site control
CBB

Ron Pakker

Contractor
Friso Bouwgroep

Pier Zwerver
John uit Oude Groeneveld
Gerard Siemensma

Technical systems
Nelissen Ingenieursbureau b.v.

Frank van Leersum
Stan van Alphen

Structural engineering
Van Rossum Ingenieursgroep

Anne van der Sluis
Mike Tromp

Costing
BBN adviseurs

In the beginning of the design process various study models were developed which would lead to the final design. The study models investigate the primary design decisions such as the passengers flow from car to plane, the site characteristics and the combination of a GA terminal with offices.

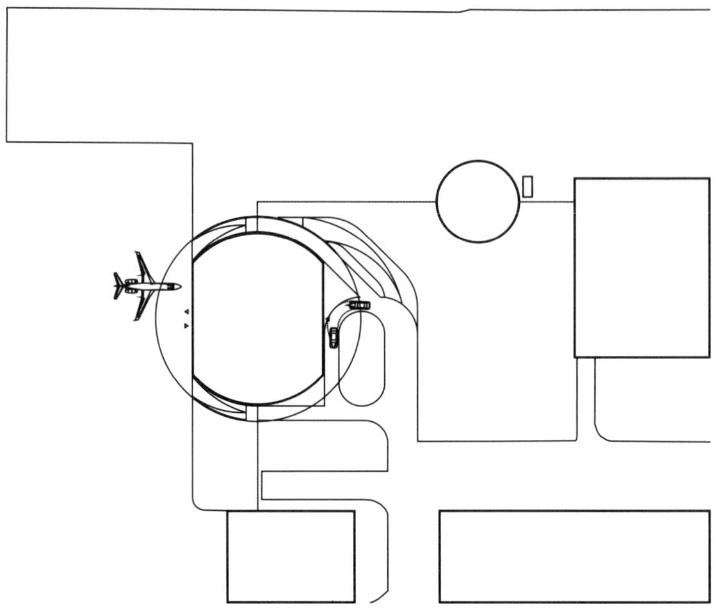

fig. 1) Study model 1 (Round form)

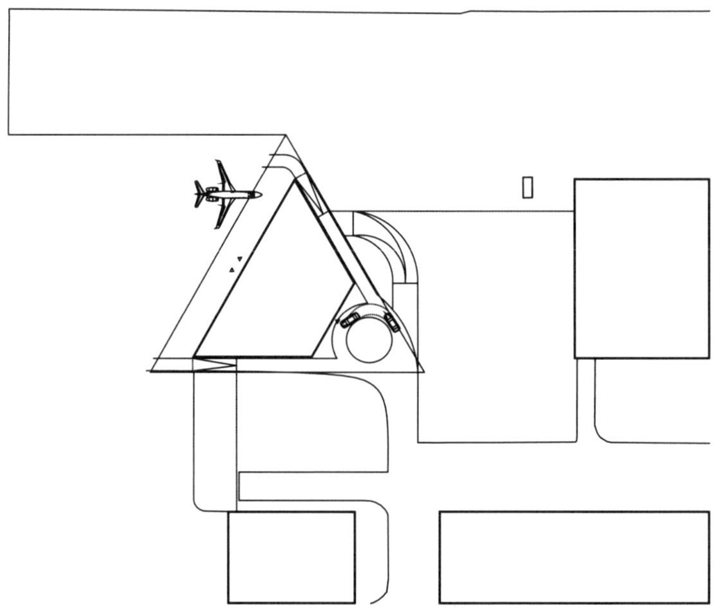

fig. 2) Study model 2 (Triangular)

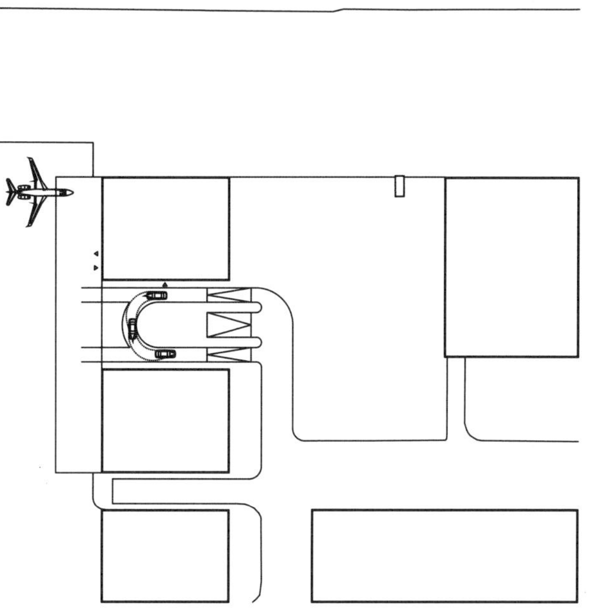

fig. 3) Study model 3 (Drive-through)

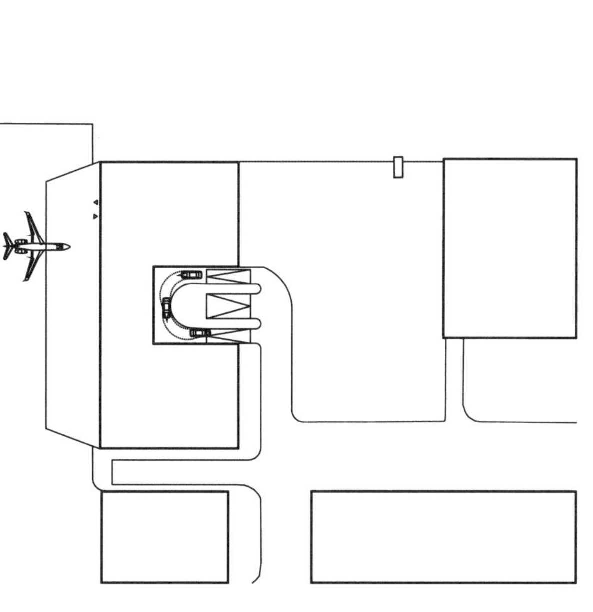

fig. 4) Plan of the built version as it is today.

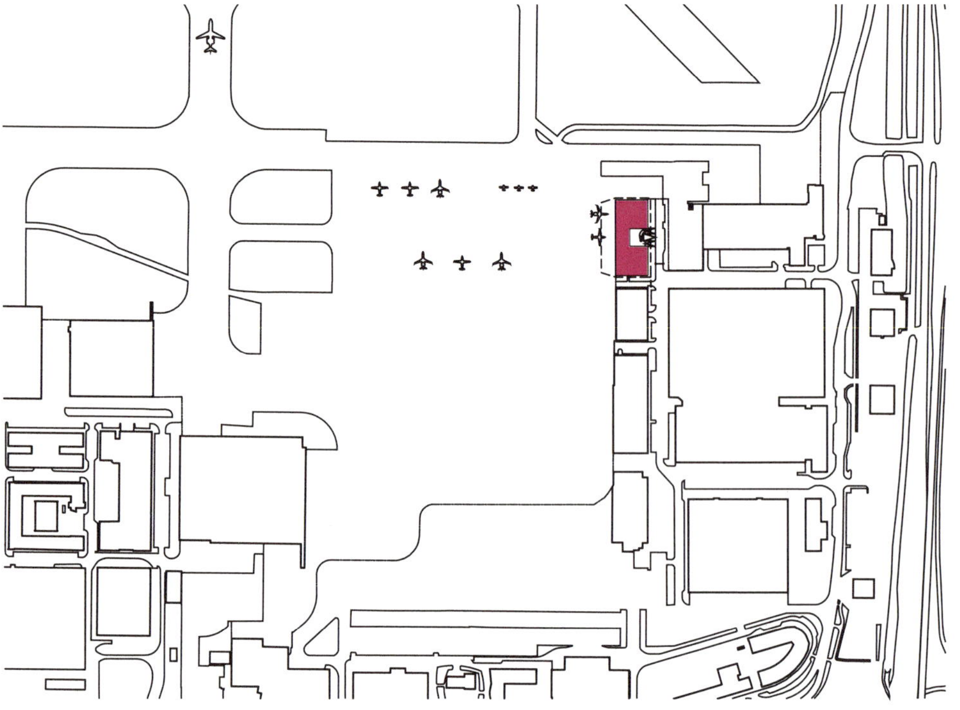

fig. 5) Site plan

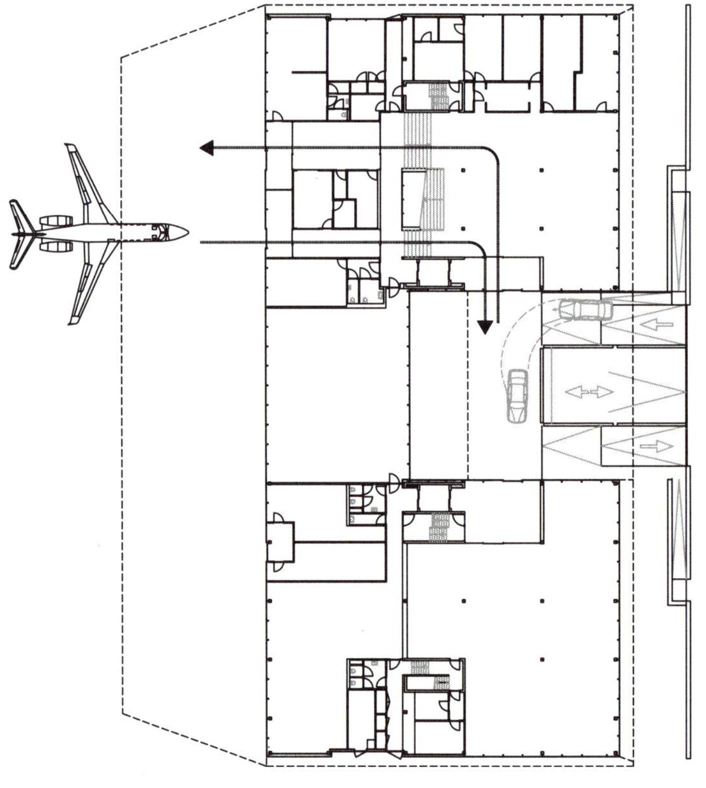

fig. 6) Ground floor with the the passengers flow of the terminal

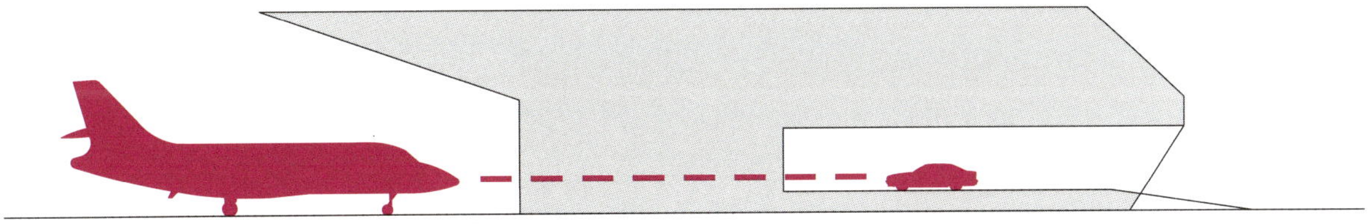

fig. 7) Concept diagram showing the plane and car brought together in and under the building.

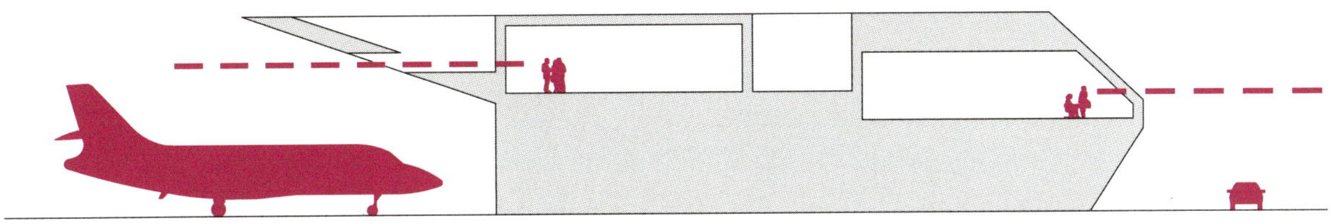

fig. 8) Concept diagram showing how the shape provides privacy to arriving and departing passengers.

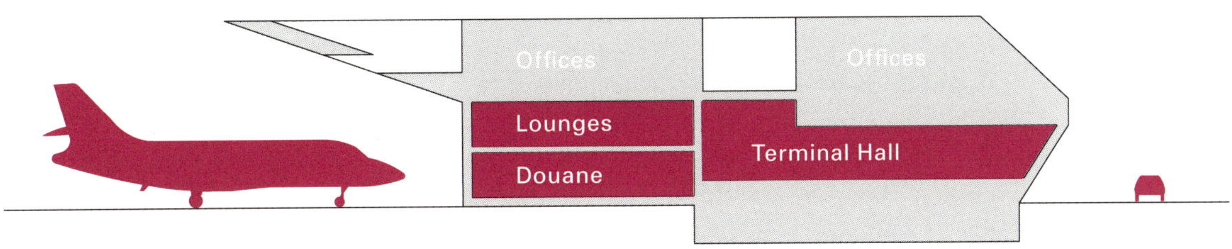

fig. 9) Concept diagram explaining the split-level and organisation of the terminal.

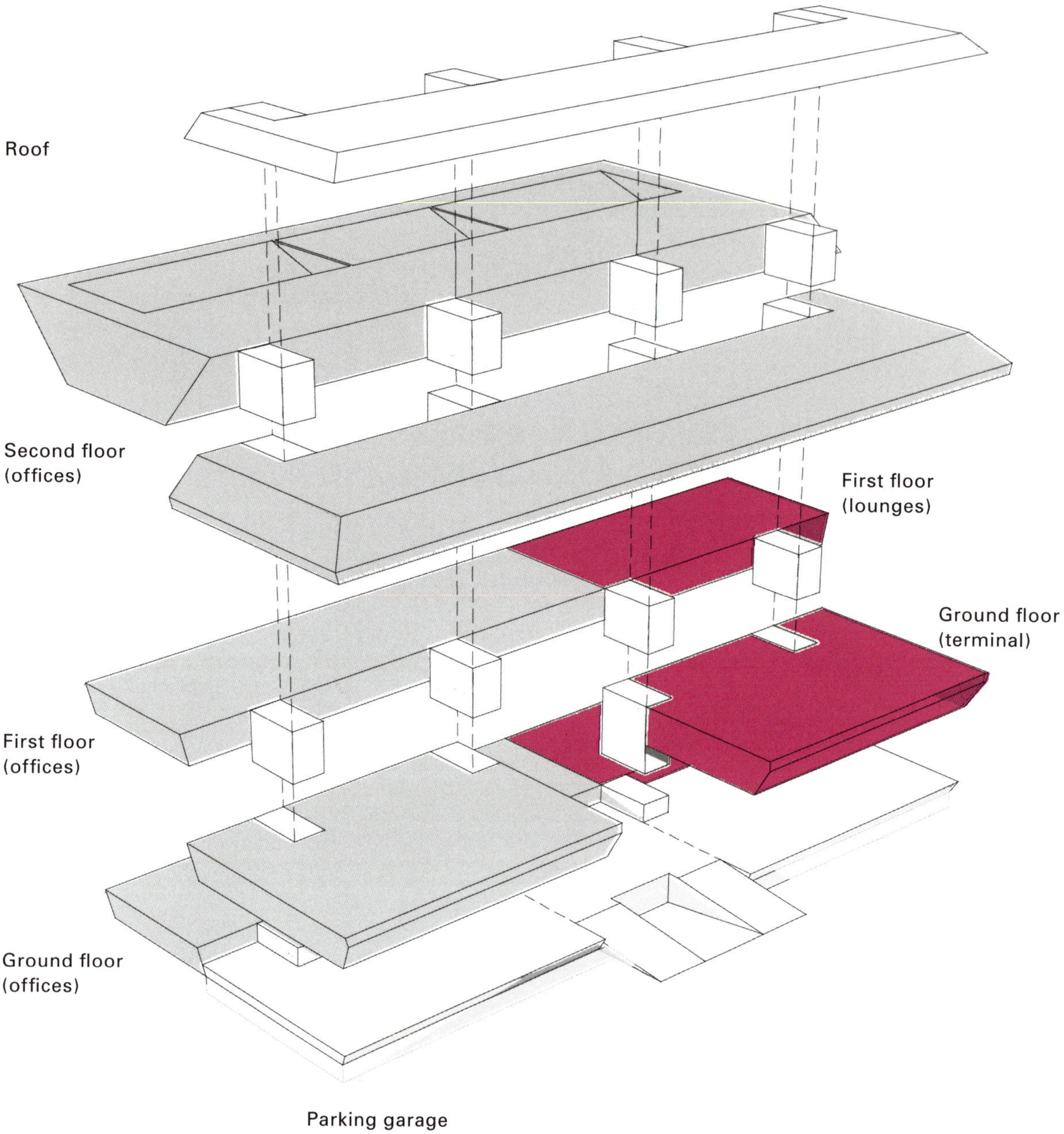

fig. 10) Isometric drawing explaining the organisation and split level of the building.

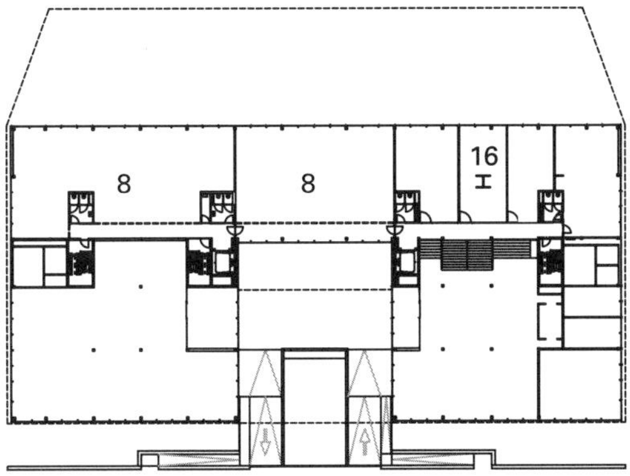

First floor

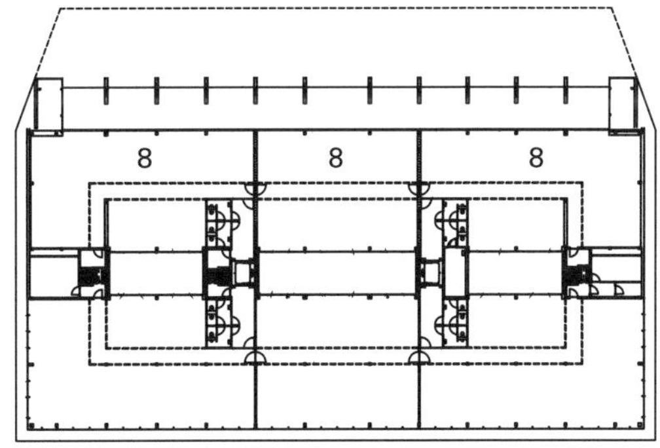

Second floor

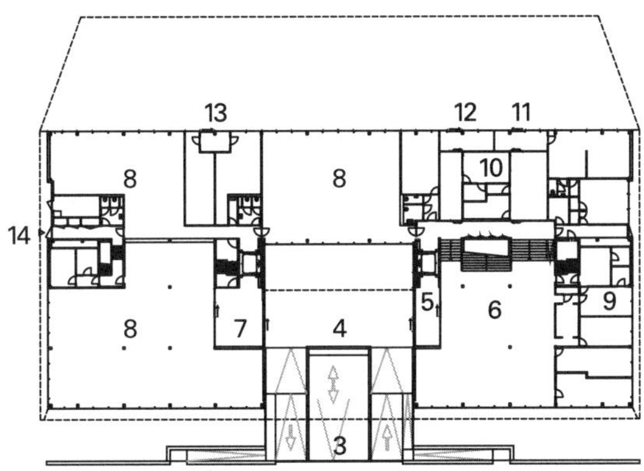

Ground floor

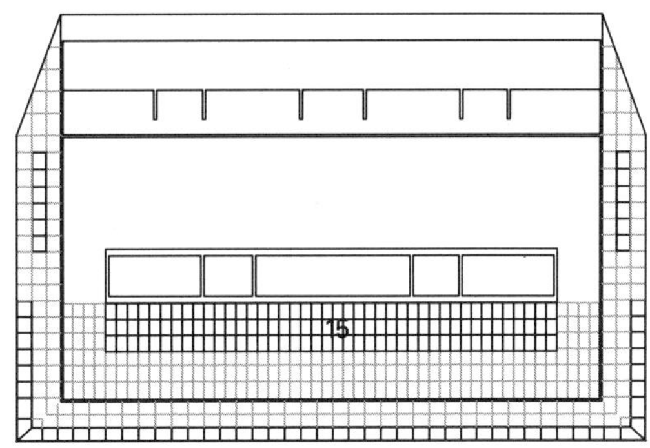

Roof

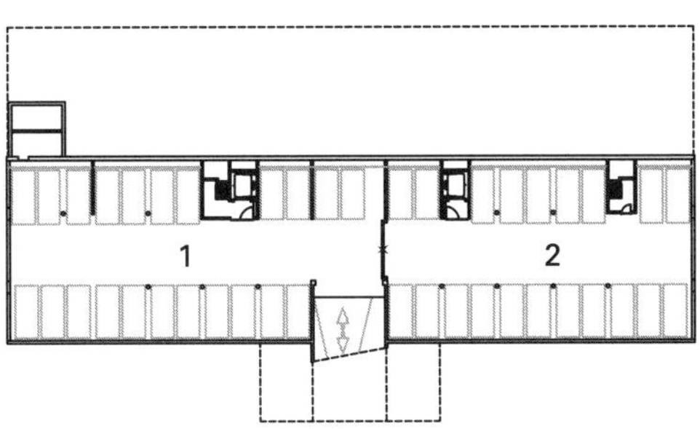

Parking garage

fig. 11) Floorplans

1 office parking
2 terminal parking
3 entrance garage
4 drive-in
5 entrance terminal
6 terminal hall
7 entrance offices
8 offices
9 terminal back-office
10 security filter
11 departures
12 arrivals
13 platform staff
14 staff entrance
15 technical installations
16 VIP lounges

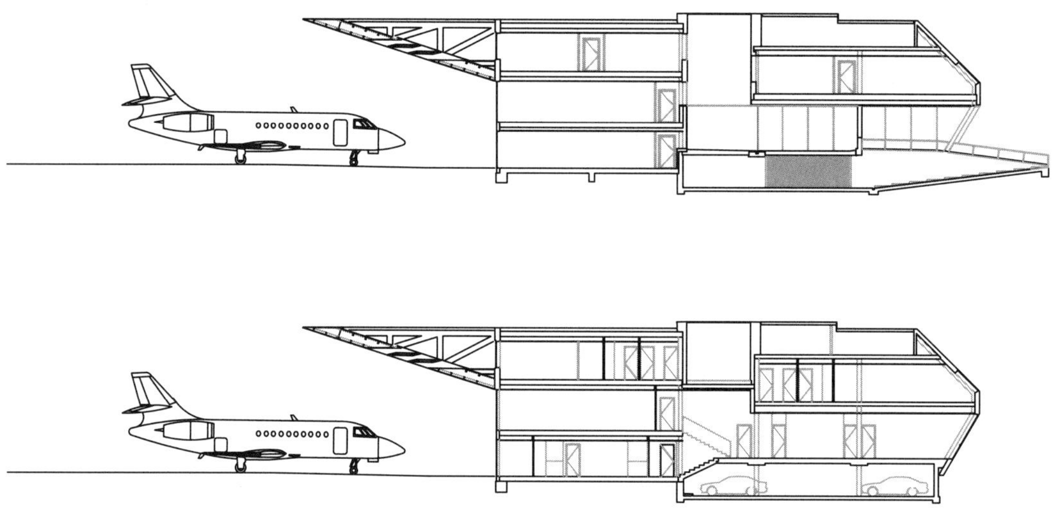

fig. 12) Cross sections

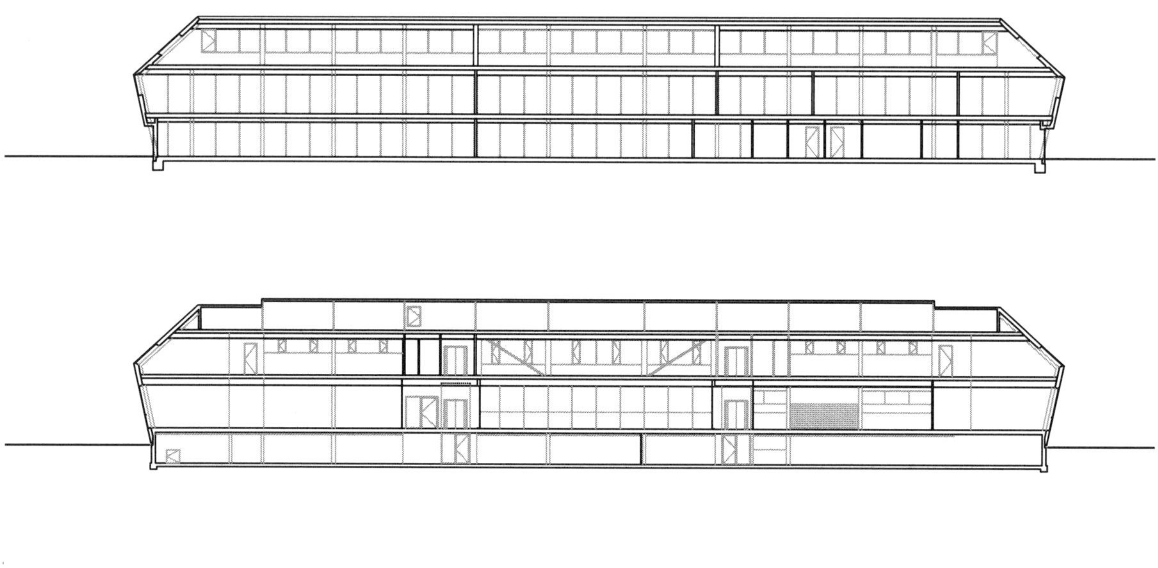

fig. 13) Longitudinal sections

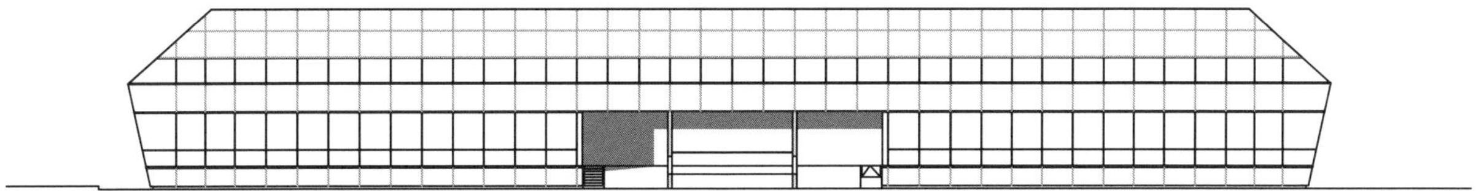

Northeast elevation

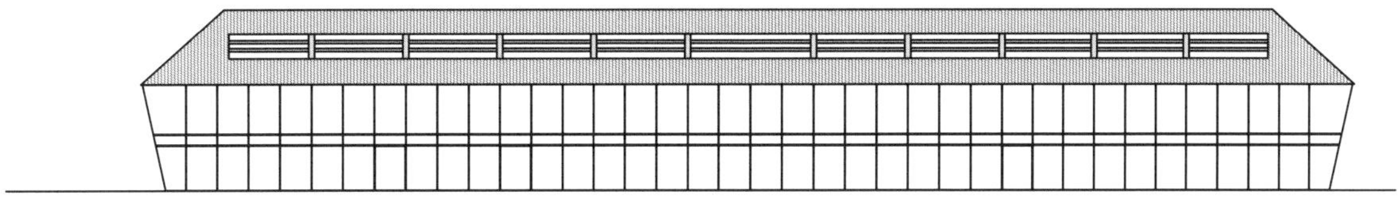

Southwest elevation

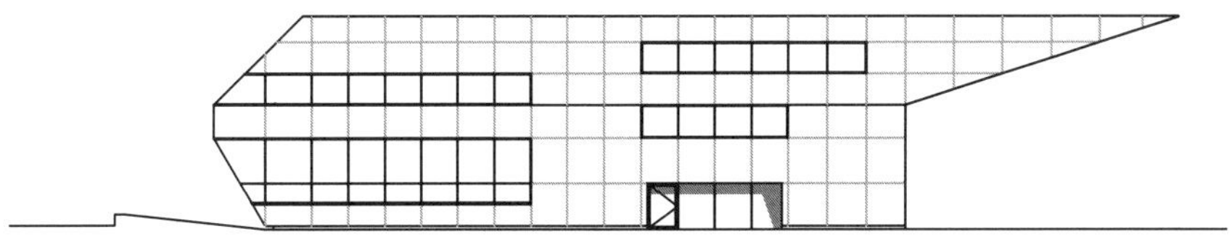

Northwest elevation

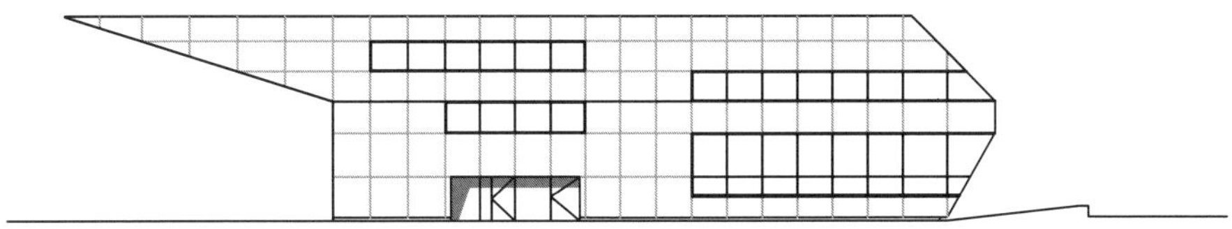

Southeast elevation

fig. 14) Facades

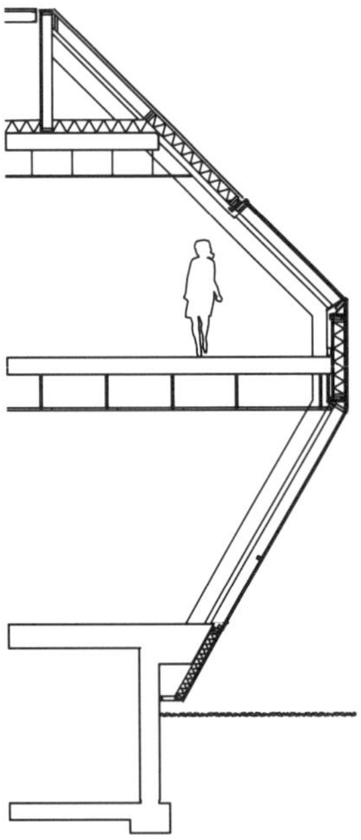

fig. 15) Detailed section of the building on landside

fig. 16) The steel columns placed on site showing the characteristic angles of the buildings for the first time.

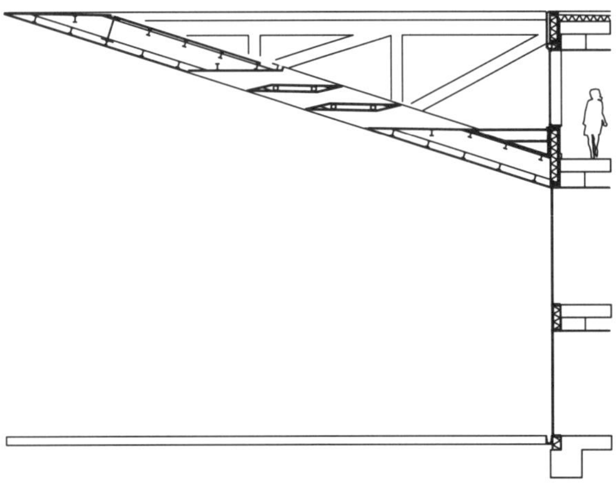

fig. 17) Detailed section of the building on airside

fig. 18) The steel structure of the canopy completed.

30/10/2009

Site on the day when the construction contract was signed

08/12/2009

First foundation piles being driven into the ground at night

05/01/2010

Unworkable day due to winter weather

03/02/2010

Groundwork for basement (parking garage)

03/02/2010

Foundations of ground floor on airside in progress

16/03/2010

Concrete floor of the parking garage being poured

30/03/2010

Ground floor on airside under construction

19/04/2010

First entrance of the building is visible: the parking garage

18/05/2010

The ground floor on landside finished and concrete cores going up

20/05/2010

All concrete cores for stairs and elevators clearly visible from airside

01/06/2010

Starting day for the assembly of the steel structure on site

02/06/2010

Second day for the assembly of the steel structure on site

04/06/2010

First phase of the steel struture on landside is finished

10/06/2010

Work on first floor and secondary supporting steel structure

14/06/2010

Steel structure being stabilised after placing of concrete floors

22/06/2010

Second phase of steel structure on airside in preperation for assembly

22/06/2010

Preparations for the second phase of steel structure on airside

24/06/2010

Building seen from above showing the two different construction phases

02/07/2010

Steel truss for the support of the canopy being installed

09/07/2010

Work in progress on the building with a jet being refueled on the background

13/07/2010

Inside the stairs of the terminal hall have been installed

22/07/2010

On the platform a three-dimensional truss for the corner of the canopy

23/07/2010

Both construction phases reach the same height

17/08/2010

The supporting structure for the cladding of the canopy is installed

01/09/2010

The building officially reached its highest point

02/09/2010

Work on the canopy construction continues the next day

14/09/2010

First glass placed on airside facade

17/09/2010

Landside facade before windows and facade were finished

18/02/2011

Temporary tent allowing the appropriate conditions to fix the facade panels

03/05/2011

The facades are finished, work on terrain, interior are still in progress

14/06/2011

The new platform infront of the building is finished

11/07/2011

First flight from the new General Aviation Terminal

CVs

Schiphol Real Estate

Schiphol Real Estate, a full subsidiary of Schiphol Group, develops, manages, operates and invests in property at and around airports in the Netherlands and abroad. The company has played an important role in the development and construction of Amsterdam Airport Schiphol. The portfolio consists of operational and commercial property with one connecting theme, the presence of an international airport.

Schiphol Real Estate has a clear vision about airport real estate. For Schiphol Real Estate, airports are more than just places to board and disembark from planes. An airport is like a modern city – not one that has come into being in the way that Amsterdam or New York has, but one that has been designed. Yet airports are also very different from modern cities in that they do not have any inhabitants. Airport City is not just an experience, it is a formula: Schiphol Real Estate's vision of what airports should be.

Schiphol Real Estate is one of the most important leaders in this niche market. The company has a unique knowledge and expertise in the field of commercial real estate that is combined with experience on the complexity of airports and airport processes and an own vision of landscaping, infrastructure, airport real estate and urban planning. The mission of Schiphol Real Estate is to create 'preferred locations': inspiring business environments that originate from a clear, customer-centric and spatial-planning perspective as well as from the complex functions and high ambitions of an airport. It does so with a focus on new trends and changing customer demands. The key elements are flexibility, connectivity, multifunctionality, dynamics and experience, and value for money.

The best showcase of Schiphol Real Estate is Amsterdam Airport Schiphol itself, one of the biggest and best-organized airports in Europe. The airport area provides the service level of a major city to around 45 million travellers a year, 60,000 workers, 540 companies and 1,500,000 square feet of office and warehouse space (terminal building excluded).

Schiphol Real Estate is active at Amsterdam Airport Schiphol and Eindhoven Airport, Rotterdam The Hague Airport, Milan Malpensa Airport and Hong Kong International Airport.

VMX architects

VMX Architects is an internationally-oriented architectural firm based in Amsterdam and Basel. The combination of innovative designs with efficient service is what best characterizes their work. VMX sees architecture as an applied art, and innovation is an inseparable part of that.

Since its founding in 1995, the firm has been headed by Don Murphy (Cork, 1965), the creative director, and Leon Teunissen (Heerlen, 1965), the business director. Murphy studied at Southbank University in London and the Berlage Institute in Amsterdam. Teunissen specialized in Architecture and Building Management at TU Delft. The firm consists of a team that can handle the entire design process from concept to completion.

VMX strives for a broad portfolio, and over the past sixteen years has completed more than thirty buildings. The assignments vary in scope and nature, ranging from urban development to interiors, but always with a strong emphasis on buildings. In addition to the VIP terminal at Schiphol and the bike rack next to Amsterdam Central Station, VMX has realized housing projects, care institutions, offices, hotels, commercial properties and schools. It has also designed buildings in Switzerland, Belgium, Ireland, Korea and China. VMX's work has been written up in international publications and has been awarded numerous prizes.

VMX focuses on the value of a building in the future, for the owner, users and surroundings. Sustainability, similarly to construction techniques or cost containment, for example, is considered a integral part of the design process. When designing, VMX continually puts itself in the position of the user. Without explicitly striving to create eye-catching buildings, the designs are extremely distinct and recognizable.

With every assignment, VMX searches for the essence of the project (often not verbalized by the client) and uses it to focus the concept of the design. This may involve particularly considering the user's comfort for instance, but could also be the views, or the building's relationship with its surroundings. For every assignment, VMX seeks and develops a typology that supports the concept of the project. This is also used as a guiding factor for the design's further elaboration and materialization. Focusing on the essence of the assignment and enlarging it leads to extremely functional and recognizable buildings.

Murphy and Teunissen are also involved in educational activities at various academies and universities. Teunissen regularly publishes texts on management and entrepreneurship and Murphy is supervisor for Sloterdijk on behalf of the City of Amsterdam.

Dutch Translation

GA Terminal Schiphol maakt van vliegen weer een magische belevenis

Marina de Vries

Glamoureus en zakelijk

Het is een opmerkelijke verschijning, de General Aviation Terminal Schiphol, waar de privé- en zakenvluchten van staatshoofden, CEO's, leden van het Koninklijk Huis, popsterren, topvoetballers en sportvliegers worden afgehandeld. Geraffineerd voegt de terminal zich in de zakelijk-chique en industriële omgeving van Schiphol-Oost. Tegelijk onderscheidt de terminal zich van de omliggende bedrijven en hangars door te stralen van vliegplezier. Zo karakteristiek is de nieuwe, bescheiden terminal dat hij zelfs vanuit zijn grote broer op Schiphol-Centrum opvalt: vanwege zijn gestroomlijnde vorm en zijn magentakleurige luifel, vanwege zijn als een discobal glinsterende beplating en zijn warmroze gloed in de avondzon. Niet alleen is de GA Terminal Schiphol een glamoureus gebouw, hij bevrijdt ook alle bij het vliegen horende handelingen uit hun harnas van routine en noodzakelijk kwaad. Gedaan is het met de oneliner 'Zitten is een werkwoord' van de beroemde Nederlandse architect Gerrit Rietveld (1888–1964). In deze GA Terminal worden alle grondfuncties – aankomen, voorrijden, parkeren, inchecken, wachten, zitten, wegtaxiën – verheven tot magische belevenissen.

Of het er nu om gaat dat je via de drive-in voor komt rijden zonder last te hebben van regen of paparazzi, of dat je in een van de lounges zit te wachten, die zich op hetzelfde niveau bevinden als de cockpit van je eigen vliegmachine. Of dat je het contrast beleeft tussen de mysterieus spiegelende buitenkant van de terminal en het weidse uitzicht dat je van binnen hebt, of dat je in de roze spiegelramen een vliegtuigsilhouet dat landt of opstijgt ziet dansen – de handelingen rijgen zich aaneen als scènes in een film. Daarmee nestelt GA Terminal Schiphol zich in het geheugen.

Niet alleen aan de passagiers, ook aan de piloot is gedacht. Terwijl die in zijn eigen, half verzonken domein zit te wachten, onttrokken aan het oog, ziet hij zijn gasten al van verre aankomen.

Multifunctionele terminal voor meerdere afhandelaren

General Aviation – met Piaggio's, Gulfstreams en Learjets voor maximaal twintig passagiers – mag in Amerika met zijn talrijke miljonairs de gewoonste zaak van de wereld zijn, in Nederland is het een stabiele nichemarkt. Deze exclusieve sector telt zo'n 15.000 vluchten en 45.000 passagiers per jaar, een fractie van de 400.000 vluchten en 45 miljoen passagiers per jaar van de reguliere luchtvaart op Schiphol. Doorgaans is een GA Terminal een relatief klein gebouw, dat eruitziet als een chic kantoor. Nieuwbouw wordt er, zeker in Europa, zelden voor gepleegd.

Op Amsterdam Airport Schiphol zetelde de General Aviation tot juli 2011 in Gebouw 106, een onderdeel van de voormalige, naoorlogse hoofdterminal dat bleef staan toen de hoofdluchthaven eind jaren zestig van Schiphol-Oost naar Schiphol-Centrum verhuisde. Sindsdien ontwikkelt Schiphol-Oost zich tot een hoogwaardige campus, bestaande uit kantoren, hotels en hangars waarin het technisch onderhoud aan vliegtuigen wordt uitgevoerd.

Zo'n vijftien jaar geleden ontstond behoefte aan nieuwbouw van de GA Terminal, omdat het oude gebouw inefficiënt en sleets was geworden. Er waren zelfs plannen om dit segment naar elders te verplaatsen. Maar de samenleving en het bedrijfsleven internationaliseerden rond de eeuwwisseling sterk en het belang van de sector nam aanzienlijk toe. En daar hoort een goed functionerende GA Terminal bij. Op basis van interviews met afhandelaren en operators kwam vastgoedonderneming Schiphol Real Estate, dat commercieel vastgoed ontwikkelt, beheert en investeert op Schiphol en een aantal andere internationale luchthavens, tot de conclusie dat nieuwbouw in dit geval wel haalbaar was. Maar dan alleen nieuwbouw van een uniek gebouwtype: een multifunctionele terminal: een terminal voor meerdere afhandelaren met kantoren, showrooms en parkeerfaciliteiten.

Verlangen naar vliegmagie

Met de functies en de verlangens van de doelgroep in het achterhoofd nodigde Schiphol Real Estate drie Nederlandse architectenbureaus uit om hun visie te geven op een nieuwe GA Terminal. De keuze viel uiteindelijk op VMX Architects. Dit in Amsterdam gevestigde bureau had toen al een aantal bijzondere gebouwen opgeleverd. Naast woonhuizen en scholen trokken vooral de tijdelijke fietsenstalling naast het Amsterdamse Centraal Station en het knalpaarse kantoorgebouw van de Rijksgebouwendienst Directie Noordzee in Rijswijk de aandacht. De gebouwen van VMX zijn gebruikersvriendelijk, functioneel en sensationeel. Toch is het architectenbureau niet zozeer gekozen vanwege zijn bijzondere ontwerpen als wel vanwege zijn conceptmatige denken. Naar 'een dergelijke aanpak was Schiphol Real Estate op zoek, want het eisenpakket voor de GA Terminal moest in dialoog met de gebruikers worden ontwikkeld. Daarnaast had VMX aansprekende ideeën: men wilde terug naar de opwinding en de glamour van de Golden Age van de luchtvaart – de jaren vijftig en zestig van de vorige eeuw, toen de toename van de hoeveelheid vrije tijd en welvaart gepaard ging met een snelle groei van het vliegverkeer. Zelfs een bezoek aan het luchthavenrestaurant was in die tijd al een sensatie. In de bestaande GA Terminal was die vliegmagie, zoals in vele terminals tegenwoordig, achter een waaier van veiligheidsmaatregelen naar de achtergrond gedrongen. Bovendien kampte het gebouw met een aantal andere gebreken, waaronder lange vervoerslijnen voor de passagier. Die moest per bus van de terminal naar zijn vliegtuig worden getransporteerd.

Zo kwam het eisenpakket langzaam maar zeker op tafel. De nieuwe GA Terminal moest een toonbeeld zijn van vliegplezier, een glamoureus, gastvrij en comfortabel gebouw, met minimale loopafstanden en maximale privacy. Tot in de kantoren moest de sensatie van het vliegen voelbaar zijn. Voor deze wensen was de locatie – op de kop van de landingsbaan – een cadeau.

Nederlands ontwerptalent als visitekaartje

Aan de basis van de GA Terminal ligt een zoektocht: naar de geschiedenis van de locatie en naar spraakmakende terminalarchitectuur uit binnen- en buitenland. Schiphol is altijd een innovatieve koploper geweest. In 1938 was Schiphol een van de eerste luchthavens van Europa met een verhard banenstelsel. In de naoorlogse jaren groeide de luchthaven op Schiphol-Oost uit tot de rode loper van Nederland. Daar arriveerden de beroemdheden en leden van het Koninklijk Huis, van filmster Jayne Mansfield en dominee Martin Luther King tot prins Bernhard. Het publiek keek toe vanaf spectaculaire dakterrassen.

Schiphol-Centrum maakte vanaf zijn ingebruikname in 1967 furore als een van de eerste passagiersvriendelijke luchthavens van de wereld. Dat had vooral te maken met de hoofdterminal van architect Marius Duintjer (1908–1983) en NACO (Nederlandse Airport Consultants). Die terminal was uitermate functioneel, overzichtelijk en elegant, licht en transparant als een doorzonwoning, en gebaseerd op de menselijke maat. Het interieur was op maat gemaakt door Ko Liang Ie en de heldere bewegwijzering van Benno Wissing, waarbij gele borden de vitale richtingen aangaven voor de passagier, was een voorbeeld voor tal van luchthavens. Ook de latere uitbreiding van de bewegwijzering, een vernieuwend ontwerp van Paul Mijksenaar met pictogrammen, krijgt wereldwijd nog steeds navolging.

Nog altijd zet Schiphol Nederlands ontwerptalent in om de luchthaven te markeren als toegangspoort van Nederland, in samenwerking met architectenbureaus als cepezed, Benthem Crouwel, Paul de Ruiter, Quist Wintermans en Broekbakema. Werk van hedendaagse kunstenaars als Rob Birza, Tom Claassen en John Körmeling dat op Schiphol wordt tentoongesteld, biedt verstrooiing en inspiratie.

Tegenwoordig maakt de luchthaven naam als AirportCity, een levendige stad met een mix aan functies, van de terminal tot in de business parks die in de afgelopen decennia zijn ontwikkeld. De dependance van het Rijksmuseum achter de paspoortcontrole, de onlangs in gebruik genomen Airport Library en Airport Park zijn uniek. Meer en meer 'Dutch Design' wordt op Schiphol toegevoegd. Maar hoezeer de Nederlandse hoofdluchthaven ook blijft vernieuwen, de terminal van Duintjer staat bij architecten, ook bij VMX, in het geheugen gegrift.

Vliegtuig voor de deur

Het ontwerpteam van de GA Terminal – behalve VMX Architects en Schiphol Real Estate zijn dat constructeur Van Rossum en installatieadviseur Nelissen, voor het bouwen uitgebreid met aannemer Friso Bouwgroep – heeft ook naar terminals in het buitenland gekeken. Wie de Golden Age van de luchtvaart wil laten herleven, komt onherroepelijk uit bij de markante terminals van de van oorsprong Finse bouwmeester Eero Saarinen (1910–1960): de TWA Terminal van Kennedy Airport in New York en de terminal van Dulles International Airport in Chantilly, Virginia, beide in 1962 in gebruik genomen. Deze terminals vieren de vrijheid van het vliegen in expressieve, vloeiende gebouwen. Naar buiten waaierende raampartijen bieden een panoramisch uitzicht. Vooral de schuine vorm van de ramen en de relatie met het omliggende luchtvaartlandschap keren al dan niet met opzet terug in de GA Terminal.

In essentie is de nieuwe GA Terminal allereerst schatplichtig aan de villa van John Travolta in Florida. De Pulp Fiction-filmster woont in Jumbolair Aviation Estates bij Ocala, een speciale gemeenschap met huizen rond een landingsbaan. Travolta's huis heeft een drive-in voor auto's aan de ene kant en twee 'carports' voor vliegtuigen aan de andere kant. Het comfort van dit vliegtuighuis, waar de passagiers dankzij drive-in en luifels beschut tegen regen en zon hun vliegtuig kunnen betreden, werd een van de belangrijkste uitgangspunten voor de GA Terminal.

Voor de vorm van de luifel van de GA Terminal hebben echter andere terminals model gestaan: de grootse, elegante luifel rondom de Pan Am Terminal op JFK Airport in New York ontworpen door Ives, Turano & Gardner Associated Architects en Walter Prokosch van Tippetts-Abbett-McCarthy-Stratton (1960), waaronder de vliegtuigen met hun neus richting terminal staan geparkeerd, en de halfcirkelvormige, veertig meter lange overdekking van Berlin Tempelhof (1937) van Ernst Sagebiel, met zijn destijds uiterst moderne, aan een vliegtuigvleugel refererende metaalconstructie.

Tot in detail op maat gemaakt

Hoe inspirerend het ontwerp ook is, geen enkele bestaande terminal biedt een pasklaar antwoord voor de specifieke opgave van de GA Terminal van Schiphol. Die is langzaam maar gestaag op maat geboetseerd en op zijn locatie verankerd, en is daarmee met het voordeel van de terugblik een toonbeeld van slow architecture. Daarbij wordt weer aandacht gevraagd voor in hun plek wortelende, herkenbare en met toewijding gemaakte gebouwen.

Vanuit het wensenpakket van privacy, comfort, efficiency en openheid naast magie en glamour, maar zonder nostalgie, diende zich al snel een aantal bouwkundige oplossingen aan. Onder een royale luifel zou het vliegtuig met zijn neus tot vlak bij de terminal kunnen worden geparkeerd, en de combinatie met een drive-in zou ervoor zorgen dat de passagiers droog en uit het zicht van nieuwsgierige blikken kunnen in- en uitstappen. Door de transparante split-level-opzet staan zo veel mogelijk ruimtes – lounges, terminal, paspoortcontrole en kantoren – in directe verbinding met het vliegspektakel aan airside, terwijl de loopafstanden voor de passagiers minimaal zijn. Doordat de terminal open en vrij is gehouden, hebben zowel passagiers als afhandelaren een goed overzicht, waardoor het aantal bewakingscamera's tot een minimum kon worden beperkt. Er zijn wel camera's aanwezig, maar net als de overige veiligheidsmaatregelen vallen ze geheel niet op.

Het sculpturale exterieur kwam minder snel tot stand. In de eerste studies was de GA Terminal rond, net zoals andere ontwerpen van VMX en zoals JFK Airport. Een tweede studie leverde een vierkant ontwerp op, met een kaarsrechte luifel en een uitstekend staketsel als drive-in. Maar het ontwerp bleek geen lonende exploitatie mogelijk te maken. Om aan de financiële voorwaarden te kunnen voldoen koos men voor een onorthodoxe oplossing. Het gebouw is niet verkleind, maar vergroot: er kwam meer kantoorruimte voor de afhandelaren en andere geïnteresseerde partijen. Maar daarmee werd de logistieke puzzel, toch al ingewikkeld vanwege de combinatie van aviation en non-aviation, nog complexer. Want hoe kon de zozeer gewenste privacy van de passagiers worden gewaarborgd nu smartphones van ons allen paparazzi maken? Om direct zicht vanuit de bovenliggende kantoren op de vliegtuigparking te verhinderen is de luifel schuin omhoog getild. Lange, open stroken in de luifel zorgen voor daglicht in de kantoren en voor een enerverend uitzicht op het omringende luchtvaartlandschap, ook vanaf de bureaustoel. Om vierkante meters te winnen binnen de voorgeschreven rooi- en hoogtelijnen zijn de wanden van het gebouw aan drie zijden schuin naar buiten geduwd, met aan Saarinen herinnerende raampartijen als resultaat. Zo groeide het ontwerp uit tot een dynamisch en karakteristiek driedimensionaal wybertje, tot in detail op maat gemaakt.

Luifel als roze loper

Zoals de opmerkelijke vorm vanuit de opgave is ontstaan, zo zijn ook de kleuren en de materialen tot stand gekomen. Beide moesten eenvoudig en zakelijk overkomen, passend bij de locatie, maar ook sensueel, glamoureus en onderscheidend zijn. Grijs en glanzend is de eerste aanblik van het gebouw, in overeenstemming met de aluminiumkleur die het masterplan van Benthem Crouwel voor Schiphol voorschrijft. Daarbij knipoogt het grijs van de GA Terminal vrolijk naar zijn omgeving. Het speciaal ontwikkelde paneelsysteem heeft spikkels als een discobal. Bij mooi weer vliegen de kleuren in het rond. Zilvergrijs is ook het spiegelglas van de royale schuine ramen aan landside. Dat spiegelglas houdt nieuwsgierige blikken buiten en zorgt voor privacy. Tegelijk versterkt het de dynamiek van de terminal door de grootse, Hollandse wolkenluchten en de opwindende skyline van het luchthavenlandschap te weerkaatsen als in een voortdurend veranderend schilderij.

Maar het is de bepaald ongebruikelijke kleur magenta van de luifel en de airside-raampartij die de GA Terminal zo herkenbaar maakt. De vraag is waarom men voor deze kleur heeft gekozen. Een reden komt zelden alleen. Voor de luifel wilde Schiphol Real Estate een voor Schiphol unieke kleur, een roodtint, om de uitzonderingspositie van de terminal te onderstrepen en om de terminal vanaf Schiphol-Centrum goed zichtbaar te maken. De kleur rood is gebaseerd op de rode loper waarmee vips internationaal welkom worden geheten. Het werd magenta, een mix van het kosmopolitisme van de cocktail Cosmopolitan*, van de zakelijkheid van *Het Financieele Dagblad* en de sportiviteit van de Giro d'Italia.

Rozerood is ook de kleur van girl glamour, en hiermee neemt de terminal een voorschot op de toekomst. Dan zal de General Aviation niet langer vooral een mannenwereld zijn. Vrouwen zijn steeds beter vertegenwoordigd op hoge zakelijke posities, en vormen een belangrijke doelgroep van de General Aviation. De GA Terminal op Schiphol heet hen alvast welkom: ook bij Hollands grauw weer laat de roze glaswand de wereld baden in een warme gloed.

Juweel in de skyline

De GA Terminal voegt zich niet alleen geraffineerd op zijn plek, maar voegt zich ook op geheel eigen en eigentijdse wijze in de geschiedenis en de reputatie van Schiphol. De terminal is in voortzetting van het ontwerp van Duintjer overzichtelijk en efficiënt, licht en transparant, elegant en tot in de puntjes verzorgd. Net zoals een aantal buitenlandse terminals uit de Golden Age viert de GA Terminal de vrijheid en de lichtheid van het vliegen – in zijn vloeiende en dankzij de terug liggende plint zwevende vorm, in zijn aan een vliegtuigvleugel refererende luifelconstructie en zijn sensuele verweving met het luchtvaartlandschap. Hij voegt een nieuw hoofdstuk toe aan de geschiedenis van het vliegen: met zijn filmische uitgangspunt en zijn sensationele materiaalgebruik is de terminal niet alleen passagiersvriendelijk, maar biedt hij passagiers ook een unieke, met de locatie verweven experience.

Net als het exterieur ademt het op maat gemaakte interieur de sfeer van optimisme en glamour van het zorgeloze luchtvaarttijdperk, met een moderne inslag. De door VMX ontworpen balies hebben dezelfde vorm als de terminal en zijn even eenvoudig als inventief, even functioneel als kosmopolitisch: ze zijn incheckpunt en cocktailbar tegelijk. Ook de vloeren van de openbare ruimtes hebben die eigenschappen: ze hebben overal dezelfde composiettegel, maar doordat de platen recht dan wel diagonaal zijn verzaagd krijgt elke ruimte haar eigen identiteit. De vloer in de entreehal laat er geen misverstand over bestaan:

het wervelende windmolenmotief, een ode aan de geometrische grafiek van M.C. Escher (1898–1972), is Hollands met een knipoog.
De complexe ontwerppuzzel is dankzij de inzet en creativiteit van alle betrokken partijen ingenieus opgelost. De GA Terminal blinkt als een juweel in de skyline en is met 6000 vierkante meter bruto vloeroppervlak niet duurder dan een standaardkantoor. Met zijn energiezuinige installaties en aanwezigheidsdetectie heeft het gebouw het predikaat 'duurzaam ontwerp' gekregen. Opnieuw heeft het Nederlands ontwerp- en bouwvernuft zijn visitekaartje afgeleverd.

Marina de Vries is zelfstandig journalist op het gebied van architectuur en beeldende kunst. Zij werkt onder meer voor 'de Volkskrant', de 'Bond van Nederlandse Architecten', 'Hollands Diep' en het 'Virtueel Museum Zuidas'. Zij heeft meegewerkt aan tal van publicaties, waaronder recentelijk een over het AMC te Amsterdam.

*)

De Cosmopolitan is een cocktail, die populair is geworden dankzij de Amerikaanse televisieserie Sex and the City. De even glamoureuze als sensuele cocktail kan als volgt worden bereid:
- 5 cl wodka of tequila
- 3 cl cranberrysap
- 2 cl citroensap
- eventueel een scheutje triple sec
- shaken met ijs.

Image Credits

Cover photography
Jeroen Musch

p. 9–24
photography and copyright by Jeroen Musch

p. 25
top: Henk Jonker. Maria Austria Instituut
bottom: Particam. Maria Austria Instituut

p. 26
top: Henk Blansjaar. Spaarnestad Photo
bottom: Ben van Meerendonk. AHF, collection International Institute of Social History, Amsterdam

p. 27
top: Ben van Meerendonk. AHF, collection International Institute of Social History, Amsterdam
bottom: Ben van Meerendonk. AHF, collection International Institute of Social History, Amsterdam

p. 28–29
top: Frits J, Rotgans, Nederlands Fotomuseum
bottom: Frits J, Rotgans, Nederlands Fotomuseum

p. 30–31
Frits J, Rotgans, Nederlands Fotomuseum

p. 32
top: Frits J, Rotgans, Nederlands Fotomuseum
bottom: Frits J, Rotgans, Nederlands Fotomuseum

p. 33
top: courtesy, Bombardier Aerospace Inc.
bottom: courtesy, Bombardier Aerospace Inc.

p. 34
top: Petterik Wiggers, Hollandse Hoogte
bottom: Roy Tee, Hollandse Hoogte

p. 35
top: Gerard Wessels, Hollandse Hoogte
bottom: Peter Blok, Hollandse Hoogte

p. 36
photography and copyright by Jeroen Musch

p. 41
top: Ezra Stoller, Esto Photographics
bottom: Ezra Stoller, Esto Photographics

p. 42
top: unkown;
bottom: Ezra Stoller, Esto Photographics

p. 45–64
photopraphy and copyright by Jeroen Musch

p. 68–76
all illustrations by VMX architects

p. 76
photography by Hugo Kok, VMX architects

p. 77–80
photography by Hugo Kok and Ron Pakker

Colophon

Brilliant on the Skyline
General Aviation Terminal Schiphol

This book was commissioned by Schiphol Real Estate on the occasion of the opening of the General Aviation Terminal Schiphol on 21 September 2011.

Author
Marina de Vries

Photography
Jeroen Musch

Translation
Jane Bemont

Editors
Schiphol Real Estate
VMX architects

Copy editors
Lucy Klaassen, Isabelle Priest

Production
Nico Buitendijk, Ton van Lierop, SUN

Graphic Design
Felix Weigand

Printing
AD Druk, Zeist

Publisher
Martien de Vletter, SUN

Drawing credits
VMX architects

Cover
Jeroen Musch

Available through IDEA BOOKS,
Nieuwe Herengracht 11,
1011 RK Amsterdam,
The Netherlands,
tel + 31 20 6226154,
fax + 31 20 6209299,
idea@ideabooks.nl

SUN architecture, based in Amsterdam develops and publishes books on architecture, urban planning and landscape design. See: www.sunarchitecture.nl

ISBN: 9 789461 057457